THE LITTLE BOOK OF

LOST WORDS

THE LITTLE BOOK OF

LOST WORDS

COLLYWOBBLES, SNOLLYGOSTERS, *AND 86 OTHER* SURPRISINGLY USEFUL TERMS WORTH RESURRECTING

CREATOR OF HISTORY HUSTLE

JOE GILLARD

TEN SPEED PRESS
California | New York

CONTENTS

GOOD WORDS

ARE

WORTH MUCH,

AND

COST LITTLE.

George Herbert

INTRODUCTION

"... tongues, like governments, have a natural
tendency to degeneration; we have long preserved
our constitution, let us make some struggles for
our language." —SAMUEL JOHNSON

There are very few treasures that we can dig out of the
ground, dust off, and put into use as if they were brand-
new. Words, of course, are an exception. The purpose
of this book is to provide you with your very own collection of treasures, ready to be resurrected and introduced
into conversation with a delighted audience. I created
this book to meet the demands of the modern speaker
or writer to preserve language, colorfully express unique
emotions, and personally connect to a rich history with
the mere stroke of a key or vibration of the throat.

It's hard to define exactly why we love these dusty,
musty archaic words. Is it the colorful way they sound as
you speak them and hear them? Their odd specificity?
Their uniqueness? They do come in great variety. And
while some sound fit only for impressing one's noble peers
at an upper-crust Victorian ball, others sound like they
were overheard late at night in a dimly lit medieval tavern.
Some have ten equally evocative synonyms, while others
may be the only word ever crafted to define a certain

feeling. Whatever their origin, whatever their use, these words have this in common: they inevitably bring joy in their rediscovery. "There's a word for that," you will say, in countless conversations, settings, and situations.

Admittedly, we can see why some of these words faded away as the years slipped by and dictionaries were updated. I mean, do we really need a word for "a warning that one is about to throw waste out of a window"? (See gardyloo.) Perhaps not, but what enchantment there is in knowing that there is a word for it. Words, like traditions and customs, drop out of use when they go out of fashion. But unlike customs, which are tied to specific norms of their time, words can be brought back with an updated context! Practicality may chip away at our language, but the magic of the lost words in this book ought not to be forgotten.

Most, but not all, of the words in this book are English words. English has had many periods of playful linguistic experimentation—just consider the times of Chaucer, Shakespeare, and Dickens. English was formed in part by the requirements of playwrights, novelists, poets, speakers, actors, farmers, drinkers, and jokers to express themselves. English contains many simple monosyllabic words, and British English writers and speakers of the past delighted in mixing words together, or inventing them, purely for the silly way they sounded. That's why many of these words are so fun to say.

This book will expand your vocabulary, but it will also treat you to a glimpse of past lives. Time separates us from our ancestors, but careful study of history unites us with them in deep, empathetic, and relevant ways. You will see how much their lives were exactly like ours, and how much they differed. You will learn the ways in which their language can work in a modern world, if only we adjust the context of its use ever so slightly. Finally, you will learn where we've been—an essential component in guiding us toward a more expressive future.

When I created History Hustle, a publication for social media, I wanted to give history buffs a place of their own. A place full of history they can use, relate to, and see themselves in—a place that aims to make history palatable, humorous, and lively. Many history books, sites, magazines, movies, and podcasts focus on wars, violence, and politics. History Hustle aims to show that ordinary, everyday humans were there all along, with hopes, dreams, jokes, friends, lovers, and lives remarkably similar to our own. This book is an extension of that. Readers, you are encouraged to use these words often to show your knowledge and careful consideration of our history. These words are a toolkit for history buffs and word lovers alike to express themselves. Now, go off to your favorite snuggery (see page 159) and enjoy this fun trip back in time.

ABSQUATULATE

Verb | ab-*skwah*-choo-leyt | Nineteenth century. English.

TO RUN OFF WITH SOMEONE IN A HURRY. TO ABSCOND.

When Cody's mother started lecturing him about safe sex in front of his girlfriend, they had no choice but to absquatulate.

ACCISMUS

Noun | ak-*siz*-muhs | Sixteenth century. English.

A FAKE REFUSAL OF SOMETHING
YOU REALLY WANT.

Michael may be a master at accismus,
but he can't say no to pizza bagels.

ADAMITISM

Noun | *ad*-uhm-i-tiz-uhm | Nineteenth century. English.

THE SUPPORT OR PRACTICE OF NUDISM OR PUBLIC NUDITY, ESP. FOR RELIGIOUS REASONS.

Her husband had lately been practicing a casual form of adamitism around the house, creeping out the cat.

AISCHROLATREIA

Noun | ahys-kroh-luh-*trahy*-uh

Early twentieth century. English.

THE WORSHIP OF LEWDNESS AND OBSCENITY.

Nearly every online community eventually
becomes overrun with aischrolatreia.

AKRASIA

Noun | uh-*krey*-zhee-uh | Ancient Greek.

THE ACT OF KNOWING YOU SHOULDN'T BE DOING SOMETHING, BUT DOING IT ANYWAY. DELIBERATELY ACTING AGAINST GOOD JUDGMENT.

Was it akrasia for him to get drunk at his boss's kid's birthday party? Maybe, but bouncy houses aren't as fun when you're sober.

ALLOTRIOPHAGY

Noun | al-uh-tree-*ah*-fuh-jee

Nineteenth century. English. Medical terminology.

A STRONG URGE OR DESIRE TO EAT FOOD THAT IS ABNORMAL OR UNHEALTHY.

Mike claimed he ate nothing but ramen noodles and pork rinds because he was "broke" and "in college"—a poor excuse for his allotriophagy.

AMPHIGORY

Noun | *am*-fi-gohr-ee | Nineteenth century. English.

A PIECE OF WRITING THAT APPEARS TO HAVE MEANING BUT IS REALLY JUST FOOLISH NONSENSE.

His poetry was amphigory; it read like a late-night drunk text.

APANTHROPY

Noun | uh-*pan*-thruh-pee
Nineteenth century. English. Medical terminology.

A DESIRE TO BE ALONE; A DISTASTE FOR THE COMPANY OF OTHERS.

*"Sarah, your apanthropy is getting old;
you can't spend another weekend alone
with mac and cheese and romcoms."*

APROSEXIA

Noun | ap-ruh-*sehx*-ee-uh
Nineteenth century. English. Medical terminology.

A COMPLETE INABILITY TO FOCUS OR CONCENTRATE DUE TO A DISTRACTED, WANDERING MIND.

Johnson's aprosexia kept him from retaining anything from the three-hour board meeting.

AQUABIB

———————

Noun | *ahk*-wuh-bib | Nineteenth century. English.

A WATER-DRINKER. A TEETOTALER.

*Cheryl, the office aquabib, took
frequent trips to the bathroom.*

ATARAXIA

Noun | at-uh-*rak*-see-uh | Ancient Greek.

A STATE OF PEACEFUL SERENITY, CALMNESS, AND BLISS.

As soon as the kids left for school, she got into the bath, lit a candle, and let the ataraxia envelop her entirely.

BETWEENITY

Noun | bee-*tween*-i-tee | Eighteenth century. English.

BEING IN THE MIDDLE, OR
BETWEEN TWO THINGS.

*He was in a state of perfect betweenity, faced
with the choice of pizza or Chinese food.*

BLATTEROON

Noun | blat-er-*oon* | Eighteenth century. English.

A PERSON WHO TALKS OR BOASTS INCESSANTLY AND CONSTANTLY.

The blatteroon with the Bluetooth headset was a walking cliché.

BUMFODDER

Noun | *bum*-fah-der | Seventeenth century. English. Slang.

TOILET PAPER. A NEWSPAPER, MAGAZINE, OR USELESS DOCUMENT.

Clickbait is the bumfodder of the twenty-first century.

CALLIPYGIAN

Adjective | kal-uh-*pij*-ee-uhn | Eighteenth century. English.

POSSESSING BEAUTIFUL AND SHAPELY BUTTOCKS.

Her husband was mesmerized by the
callipygian dancers in the rap video.

CATLAP

Noun | *cat*-lap | Nineteenth century. Scottish.

A WEAK OR WATERED-DOWN DRINK
THAT'S SUITABLE ONLY FOR A CAT.

*The moonshine was no catlap; it tasted
like pure rubbing alcohol.*

CAUSERIE

Noun | kohz-uh-*ree*

Nineteenth century. English from French.

AN INFORMAL CHAT. A FRIENDLY, EASYGOING CONVERSATION.

Causerie with the boss was more dreadful than passing a stone.

CHARIENTISM

Noun | *keyr-ee-uhn-tiz-uhm* | Ancient Greek.

AN INSULT CONCEALED AS A FRIENDLY JOKE.

*She told him she loved his "dad bod," but he
suspected this was merely a charientism.*

COLLYWOBBLES

Noun | *cahl*-ee-wahb-uhls | Nineteenth century. English.

STOMACH PAIN OR SICKNESS FROM NERVOUS ANXIETY.

A dram of scotch before your wedding ceremony
can calm your collywobbles.

COMPEER

Noun | *kahm*-peer | Thirteenth century. Middle English.

A CLOSE COMPANION, COMRADE, OR ALLY.

When asked for help, a good compeer
doesn't ask questions.

DEWDROPPER

Noun | *doo*-drah-per | Early twentieth century. English. Slang.

AN UNEMPLOYED YOUNG ADULT WHO SLEEPS THROUGH THE DAY.

The exhausted gang of dewdroppers had played
online games until the sun came up.

DOCH-AN-DORRIS

Noun | dokh-an-*dor*-ris | Seventeenth century. Scottish.

A LAST DRINK; A PARTING DRINK; A DRINK FOR THE ROAD.

John promised the beer was just a doch-an-dorris, but five pints later, it was clear he wasn't leaving anytime soon.

DOUNDRINS

Noun | *down*-drinz | Seventeenth century. English.

AFTERNOON DRINKS.

After the divorce, Kevin was susceptible
to doundrins of white zin.

EGROTE

Verb | ee-*groht*
Eighteenth century. English.

TO PRETEND TO BE SICK.

He dramatically coughed into the phone to egrote his way out of the big PowerPoint presentation that day.

EYESERVANT

Noun | *ahy*-ser-vuhnt | Sixteenth century. English.

A PERSON WHO WORKS ONLY WHEN SOMEONE IS WATCHING.

As soon as the boss walked away, the eyeservant pulled her phone back out and started texting again.

FABULOSITY

Noun | fab-yoo-*lahs*-i-tee

Eighteenth century. English.

AN EXAGGERATED STATEMENT OR STORY THAT'S COMPLETELY MADE UP.

They loved his ridiculous stories about his nights out clubbing, even though it was all fabulosity.

FAMELICOSE

Adjective | fuh-*mehl*-i-cohse | Eighteenth century. English.

CONSTANTLY HUNGRY.

Marco's kids were famelicose, eating everything in the house except, of course, the kale salad he'd left them in the fridge.

FANDANGLE

Noun | fan-*dang*-guhl

Nineteenth century. English. American South.

A SPLENDID BUT USELESS ORNAMENT.

*Olivia's outfit was so emblazoned with fandangles,
one could hear her jingling from across the block.*

FIE

———

Interjection | fahy | Thirteenth century. Middle English.

AN EXPRESSION OF OUTRAGE, FURY, OR REPULSION.

"Fie upon you!" she shouted at the driver who stole her parking spot.

FLAPDOODLE

Noun | *flap*-doo-duhl | Nineteenth century. English.

FOOLISH AND BLATANTLY FALSE
IDEAS OR WORDS.

*Pete was so full of flapdoodle he couldn't
even remember what was true anymore.*

FLYPE

Verb | flahyp | Seventeenth century. Scottish.

TO ROLL UP YOUR SOCKS BEFORE PUTTING THEM ON. TO FOLD SOCKS INSIDE OUT IN PAIRS. TO FOLD SOMETHING BACK.

He was forty years old, but his mother still flyped his socks and laid them next to his folded underwear.

FOGO

———

Noun | *foh*-goh | Eighteenth century. English.

AN OVERPOWERING AND UNPLEASANT STENCH.

The magic of holding her newborn baby disappeared the moment she opened that diaper and the fogo escaped.

FOPDOODLE

Noun | *fahp*-doo-duhl

Eighteenth century. English.

AN INSIGNIFICANT FOOL. A BUFFOON.

The frat party was a fopdoodle fiesta of spoiled rich boys.

FROONCE

Verb | froon-ts | Eighteenth century. English.

TO FROLIC EXUBERANTLY WITH
NOISE AND ENERGY.

They would froonce through the mall holding
their frozen coffee drinks and clutch purses.

FRUMBERDLING

Noun | *frum*-berd-ling | Old English.

ADOLESCENTS, YOUTH.

The frumberdling have no respect,
work ethic, or taste in music.

FUDGEL

Verb | *fuh*-juhl | Eighteenth century.
English. Regional dialect.

TO PRETEND TO WORK WITHOUT ACTUALLY DOING ANYTHING.

"It's Friday, and I'm going to fudgel my way to the weekend."

GARDYLOO

Interjection | gahr-dee-*loo*
Seventeenth century. Scottish. Regional dialect.

A WARNING SHOUTED WHEN ONE IS ABOUT TO THROW WASTE OUT OF A WINDOW DOWN INTO THE STREET.

Brent couldn't hold it in any longer and yelled "Gardyloo!" before puking out the window of the moving car.

GONGOOZLER

Noun | gahn-*gooz*-ler

Twentieth century. English. Slang.

A PERSON WHO STARES.
A NONPARTICIPATING SPECTATOR.

Keenan was a Facebook gongoozler, always lurking, but never posting.

GRIMALKIN

Noun | gri-*mawl*-kin

Sixteenth century. English.

A CAT.

The furry grimalkin on her lap
was enough reason to stay in.

GROKE

Verb | grohk | Nineteenth century. Scottish. Dialect.

TO STARE EAGERLY AT SOMEONE WHO IS EATING, HOPING THEY'LL GIVE YOU FOOD.

Terrence had been known to groke when his dormmates would come back with Taco Bell.

HOMERKIN

Noun | *hoh*-mer-kin | Seventeenth century. English.

A MEASURE OF BEER.

*Many a problem can be solved with
a homerkin of the cold stuff.*

HONEYFUGGLE

Verb | *huhn*-ee-fuhg-uhl

Nineteenth century. English. Dialect.

TO COMPLIMENT OR FLATTER SOMEONE TO GET SOMETHING YOU WANT.

Ben wanted to play PS4 online, but had to honeyfuggle his girlfriend first.

HUMBUGGERY

Noun | *huhm*-buhg-er-ee
Nineteenth century. English.

NONSENSE OR DECEITFUL LANGUAGE OR IDEAS.

"This is fat-free? Humbuggery!"
he exclaimed, and took
another huge bite.

HUMGRUFFIN

Noun | *hum*-gruhf-in | Nineteenth century. English.

AN APPALLING, HIDEOUS, REPULSIVE PERSON.

Tyrone married a humgruffin, but she was rich.

KICKSHAW

Noun | *kik*-shah

Sixteenth century. English.

A DISH THAT LOOKS GOOD BUT IS LACKING IN SUBSTANCE.

Janessa had eaten nine courses of kickshaw, each the size of a grape, at the Michelin-starred restaurant, so on the drive home she stopped for a cheeseburger.

LATIBULATE

Verb | luh-*tihb*-yoo-leyt

Seventeenth century. English.

TO HIDE IN A CORNER.

Percival hated all the hubbub of his aunt's house, so he pulled out his phone to latibulate on the couch.

LOVE APPLE

Noun | *luhv* ap-uhl | Sixteenth century. English.

A TOMATO.

Craig knew the date was officially over when
he tried to spear a love apple in his salad
and squirted its juice all over her.

MAFFICK

Verb | *maf*-ik

Early twentieth century. English.

TO CELEBRATE IN AN EXTRAVAGANT, ROWDY MANNER.

The drunken wedding party took to the dance floor to maffick to the Electric Slide.

MAYHAP

Adverb | *mey*-hap or mey-*hap* | Sixteenth century. English.

PERHAPS, POSSIBLY.

*If he's coming over tonight, mayhap
you should clean the toilet.*

MINIKIN

Noun | *min*-i-kin | Sixteenth century. English.

A SMALL, PETITE CREATURE OR PERSON.

*Popping its head out of her purse was
a furry, drooling minikin.*

MUMPSIMUS

Noun | *muhmp*-si-muhs | Sixteenth century. English.

A STUBBORN PERSON WHO REFUSES TO CHANGE THEIR MIND DESPITE BEING PROVEN WRONG.

*Only the most stubborn mumpsimus
joins the Flat Earth Society.*

NAMELINGS

Noun | *neym*-lingz | Eighteenth century. English.

PEOPLE WHO POSSESS THE SAME NAME.

Amy and Aimee were besties and namelings, both turning around whenever that name was called out.

NINNYHAMMER

Noun | *nin*-ee-ham-er | Sixteenth century. English.

A FOOL.

Only a ninnyhammer doesn't vote.

NOTEKIN

Noun | *noht*-kin | Nineteenth century. English.

A LITTLE NOTE.

He broke up with her via electronic notekin.

OPSCHEPLOOPER

Noun | *ahp*-shep-loo-per

Early twentieth century. South African slang.

ONE WHO DEPENDS ON THE GENEROSITY OF OTHERS FOR MEALS.

Chris, the opscheplooper, always showed up at the restaurant without his wallet.

PAMPHAGOUS

Adjective | *pam*-fuh-guhs

Eighteenth century. English.

EATS EVERYTHING.

Teenagers are pamphagous little beasts.

PELF

Noun | pehlf
Fourteenth century. Middle English.

MONEY, ESP. WHEN ACQUIRED THROUGH FRAUD OR DECEIT.

The congressman accepted pelf from the oil industry in exchange for rolling back regulations.

PINGLE

Verb | *ping*-guhl | Nineteenth century. English.

TO WORK IN A USELESS, UNHELPFUL MANNER THAT ONLY INTERFERES.

Alexei made no contributions to group projects and would pingle his way to a passing grade.

POPINJAY

Noun | *pah*-pin-jay | Sixteenth century. English.

A PERSON WHO DRESSES AND ACTS WITH VANITY AND EXTRAVAGANCE.

Jayden was a popinjay who walked into class as if he were expecting the paparazzi.

PRANDICLE

Noun | *pran*-dik-uhl
Seventeenth century. English.

A SMALL MEAL.

The café was a place where you could get a gluten-free, sugar-free, dairy-free prandicle that would fill you up for about ten minutes.

PRICKMEDAINTY

Noun | *prik*-muh-dayn-tee
Sixteenth century. English. Dialect.

AN OVERLY NICE PERSON.

Even though it was after midnight, Fatima knew that Taylor—a prickmedainty who couldn't say no—would give her a ride.

QUAFFTIDE

Noun | *kwahf*-tyde | Sixteenth century. English.

THE TIME FOR DRINKING ALCOHOL.

The five-o'clock bell rang, and the quafftide began.

QUAINTRELLE

Noun | kweyn-*trell* | Nineteenth century. English.

SOMEONE WHO LIVES A LIFE FULL OF PASSION, LEISURE, AND ENJOYMENT.

On social media, everyone is a quaintrelle, with a celebrity lifestyle and endless good times.

QUANKED

Adjective | kwank'd | Nineteenth century. English.
Regional dialect.

EXHAUSTED OR FATIGUED FROM HARD WORK.

*Dave would get home from work quanked, barely
able to keep his eyes open for binge-watching
his favorite mindless reality shows.*

QUIDNUNC

Noun | *kwid*-nuhngk | Eighteenth century.
English.

A GOSSIPY OR
MEDDLESOME PERSON.

*Kai, the office quidnunc,
would spill the beans after the
first drink at happy hour.*

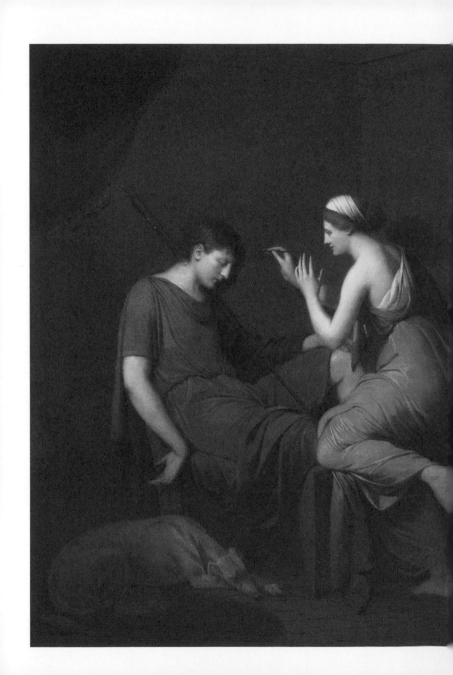

RAMFEEZLED

Adjective | ram-*feez*-uhl'd
Eighteenth century. English.

EXHAUSTED FROM A
HARD DAY OF WORK.

Millennials aren't lazy;
they're ramfeezled.

RAPSCALLION

Noun | rap-*skal*-yuhn | Seventeenth century. English.

A MISCHIEVOUS OR RASCALLY PERSON. A SCOUNDREL.

Mark was the office rapscallion, always pulling clever pranks on the diligent, butt-kissing yes men.

RIZZLE

Verb | *riz*-uhl
Nineteenth century. English.

TO RELAX AND DIGEST AFTER CONSUMING A LARGE MEAL.

Tina turned on the TV to rizzle after polishing off two boxes of mac and cheese.

SCAMBLER

Noun | *skam*-bler
Nineteenth century. Scottish.

AN UNINVITED GUEST WHO APPEARS ONLY AT MEALTIMES.

Brian's scambler "friend" was more interested in Brian's mom's cooking than he was in Brian.

SCARAMOUCH

Noun | *skair*-uh-moosh | Seventeenth century. English.

A BRAGGART WHO IS SECRETLY A COWARD.

*The scaramouch was all talk until the other man
stood up and grabbed him by the collar.*

SCIOLIST

Noun | *sahy*-uh-list | Seventeenth century. English.

ONE WHO ONLY PRETENDS TO BE KNOWLEDGEABLE ON SUBJECTS.

The internet is a wasteland of sciolists and trolls.

SHIVVINESS

Noun | *shiv*-ee-ness | Nineteenth century.
English. Regional dialect.

THE UNPLEASANT OR ITCHY FEELING THAT COMES FROM WEARING NEW UNDERWEAR.

He went into the interview confident, but
soon felt the shivviness of his new briefs
and the sweat under his collar.

SLOOM

Noun or verb | sloom | Nineteenth century. Scottish.

A LIGHT, GENTLE SLEEP.

*The marriage officially came to an end when Mackenzie
had a sloom in the middle of Diego's story.*

SLUGABED

Noun | *sluhg*-uh-bed | Sixteenth century. English.

A PERSON WHO SLEEPS IN LATER THAN IS APPROPRIATE.

*Ginny was a slugabed and once crushed
her alarm clock with a brick.*

SMATCHET

Noun | *smach*-it | Nineteenth century. Scottish.

AN ILL-MANNERED, DESPICABLE PERSON.

Don't be a smatchet; call your mother.

SNOLLYGOSTER

Noun | *snahl*-ee-gahs-ter | Nineteenth century.

English. American slang.

A DISHONEST, CORRUPT, AND UNPRINCIPLED PERSON, ESP. A POLITICIAN.

He was senior adviser to the snollygoster-in-chief.

SNOOL

Noun | snool
Eighteenth century. Scottish.

AN OBEDIENT, SUBMISSIVE PERSON WHO WILLINGLY BOWS TO AUTHORITY.

The snool worked weekends because the boss asked him to.

SNUGGERY

Noun | *snuhg*-er-ee | Nineteenth century. English.

A SMALL, COZY, SNUG PLACE.

A cat will make a snuggery out of literally any box.

SOMEWHILE

Adverb | *suhm*-wahyl | Twelfth century. English.

AT SOME OTHER TIME. SOMETIMES.

Somewhile you will accidentally hit
"reply all" when trash-talking a coworker.

SONNTAGSLEERUNG

Noun | *zohn*-tahgz-leh-roong | Early twentieth century.
German. Medical terminology.

THE DEPRESSION ONE FEELS ON SUNDAY BEFORE THE WEEK BEGINS.

Sophie's case of sonntagsleerung had gotten worse since taking that job as a crime scene cleaner.

STING-BUM

Noun | *sting*-buhm | Seventeenth century. English. Slang.

A STINGY, MEAN PERSON.

Cleatus was usually a carefree nineteen-year-old,
but when he got his paycheck he acted like
an old sting-bum out of a Dickens novel.

TOPE

———

Verb | tohp

Seventeenth century. English. Slang.

TO DRINK ALCOHOL TO EXCESS.

*He told himself he wouldn't
tope, but it was karaoke night.*

TORTILOQUY

Noun | tohr-*til*-uh-kwee | Seventeenth century. English.

IMMORAL OR DISHONEST SPEECH.

The tortiloquy at the pharmaceutical board
meeting had reached new heights.

UHTCEARE

Noun | *oot*-kee-ar-uh | Tenth century. Old English.

LYING AWAKE IN BED FEELING ANXIOUS.

Adam's state of uhtceare kept him up the night before the convention, as he worried whether his cosplay would make the grade.

ULTRACREPIDARIAN

Noun | uhl-truh-krep-i-*dair*-ee-uhn

Nineteenth century. English.

A PERSON WITH OPINIONS ON SUBJECTS BEYOND THEIR KNOWLEDGE.

The ultracrepidarians argued over the constitution as if they were legal scholars.

VERILY

Adverb | *vair*-uh-lee

Fourteenth century. Middle English.

CERTAINLY OR TRULY.

Bubba could verily be a tool.

WAGGISH

Adjective | *wag*-ish | Sixteenth century. English.

MISCHIEVOUSLY HUMOROUS.
SILLY IN A FACETIOUS WAY.

The waggish Phillip sarcastically told his mom
about all the drugs he's been doing at college.

WAMBLECROPT

Noun | *wahm*-buhl-krahpt | Seventeenth century. English.

SEVERE DIGESTIVE DISCOMFORT.

Hot sauce gave her wamblecropt, but she couldn't say no to the challenge.

ACKNOWLEDGMENTS

Thank you to the many hard-working people who helped make this book happen. First, my editor at Ten Speed Press, Lisa Westmoreland, and all the other talented people at Ten Speed who put all this together. And a huge thanks to my agent, Mark Gottlieb, at Trident Media Group, for his support, guidance, and talent from the very beginning of the project. To these people, and the other professionals who had a hand in the book, I am deeply and sincerely grateful.

To the people in my life who have cheered for me and enabled me to work on this book, I owe enormous gratitude. My wife, Nicole Persun, is my biggest source of inspiration and guidance in creative endeavors. My mother, Sue; my father, Steve; my sister, Jessica; and my longtime "compeer," Caton White, have encouraged and helped me in huge ways that I will never be able to properly repay or thank them for. I also want to thank my father-in-law, Terry Persun, for his support and business advice, and my mother-in-law, Cathy Persun, for the love and support she's shown me.

Thanks to Alan Kessler, Ken Gunn, Jeff Sanschagrin, Coleman White, Sally Davis, Marci Van Cleve, Kip Hubbard, Aaron Vallat, and the late Julie Marston, all of whom have mentored, supported, taught, influenced, and helped me personally and professionally.

ART CREDITS

p. 5, absquatulate: Pierre-Auguste Cot, detail of *The Storm*, 1880, oil on canvas, the Metropolitan Museum of Art, New York.

p. 6, accismus: Caravaggio, detail of *Supper at Emmaus (Milan)*, 1605–1606, oil on canvas, Pinacoteca di Brera, Milan, Italy.

p. 9, adamitism: Hendrick Goltzius, *The Fall of Man*, 1616, oil on canvas, courtesy National Gallery of Art, Washington, DC.

p. 11, aischrolatreia: Abraham Bloemaert, detail of *Moses Striking the Rock*, 1596, oil on canvas, the Metropolitan Museum of Art, New York.

p. 12, akrasia: Frans Hals, *Peeckelhaeringh (The Funny Drinker)*, early 1640s, oil on canvas, Gemäldegalerie Alte Meister, Dresden, Germany.

p. 15, allotriophagy: Frans Hals, detail of *Merrymakers at Shrovetide*, ca. 1616–1617, oil on canvas, the Metropolitan Museum of Art, New York.

p. 17, amphigory: Frans Hals, *Saint John the Evangelist*, ca. 1625–1628, oil on canvas, the J. Paul Getty Museum, Los Angeles.

p. 18, apanthropy: John Singer Sargent, detail of *Nonchalior (Repose)*, 1911, oil on canvas, courtesy National Gallery of Art, Washington, DC.

p. 21, aprosexia: Pierre-Auguste Renoir, detail of *Eugène Murer (Hyacinthe-Eugène Meunier, 1841–1906)*, 1877, oil on canvas, the Metropolitan Museum of Art, New York.

p. 22, aquabib: Léon Bonnat, detail of *Roman Girl at a Fountain*, 1875, oil on canvas, the Metropolitan Museum of Art, New York.

p. 25, ataraxia: Gustave Courbet, detail of *Woman with a Parrot*, 1866, oil on canvas, the Metropolitan Museum of Art, New York.

p. 26, betweenity: Master of the Story of Joseph, detail of *Joseph Interpreting the Dreams of His Fellow Prisoners*, ca. 1500, oil on wood, the Metropolitan Museum of Art, New York.

p. 29, blatteroon: Jan Ekels the Younger, detail of *The Conversation Piece (The Sense of Smell)*, probably 1791, oil on canvas, the Metropolitan Museum of Art, New York.

p. 30, bumfodder: John Ferguson Weir, detail of *The Morning Paper*, 1868, oil on canvas, the Metropolitan Museum of Art, New York.

p. 33, callipygian: William Etty (1787–1849), detail of *The Three Graces*, date unknown, oil on millboard, the Metropolitan Museum of Art, New York.

p. 34, catlap: Pieter de Hooch, detail of *A Woman and Two Men in an Arbor*, ca. 1657–58, oil on wood, the Metropolitan Museum of Art.

p. 36, causerie: Enoch Wood Perry, detail of *Talking It Over*, 1872, oil on canvas, the Metropolitan Museum of Art, New York.

p. 39, charientism: Quentin Massys, detail of *Ill-Matched Lovers*, ca. 1520–1525, oil on canvas, courtesy National Gallery of Art, Washington, DC.

p. 40, collywobbles: Jan Steen, detail of *The Lovesick Maiden*, ca. 1660, oil on canvas, the Metropolitan Museum of Art, New York.

p. 43, compeer: Sir Henry Raeburn, *The Binning Children*, ca. 1811, oil on canvas, courtesy National Gallery of Art, Washington, DC.

p. 45, dewdropper: Salvator Rosa, detail of *The Dream of Aeneas*, 1660–1665, oil on canvas, the Metropolitan Museum of Art, New York.

p. 46, doch-an-dorris: Adriaen Brouwer, detail of *The Smokers*, ca. 1636, oil on wood, the Metropolitan Museum of Art, New York.

p. 49, doundrins: Jacob van Walscapelle, detail of *Still Life with Fruit*, 1675, oil on panel, courtesy National Gallery of Art, Washington, DC.

p. 51, egrote: D. Mary Barber, detail of *A Patient at Home*, oil painting, ca. 1953, Wellcome Collection, CC BY 4.0, https://creativecommons.org/licenses/by/4.0/legalcode#s6a.

p. 53, eyeservant: Jean-Baptiste Greuze, detail of *The Laundress*, 1761, oil on canvas, the J. Paul Getty Museum, Los Angeles.

p. 54, fabulosity: Alexandre Cabanel, detail of *Florentine Poet*, 1861, oil on wood, the Metropolitan Museum of Art, New York.

p. 57, famelicose: Jan Steen, *The Dissolute Household*, ca. 1663–1664, oil on canvas, the Metropolitan Museum of Art, New York.

p. 59, fandangle: William Merritt Chase, *Carmencita*, 1890, oil on canvas, the Metropolitan Museum of Art, New York.

p. 60, fie: Benjamin West, *The Damsel and Orlando*, ca. 1793, oil on canvas, the Metropolitan Museum of Art, New York.

p. 63, flapdoodle: Frans Hals, detail of *The Smoker*, ca. 1623–25, oil on wood, the Metropolitan Museum of Art, New York.

p. 64, flype: Attributed to Ralph Earl, *Master Rees Goring Thomas*, ca. 1783–1784, oil on canvas, the Metropolitan Museum of Art, New York.

p. 67, fogo: Workshop of Andrea del Verrocchio, detail of *Madonna and Child*, ca. 1470, tempera and gold on wood, the Metropolitan Museum of Art, New York.

p. 69, fopdoodle: George Caleb Bingham, detail of *The Jolly Flatboatmen*, 1846, oil on canvas, courtesy National Gallery of Art, Washington, DC.

p. 71, froonce: Attributed to Antonio Zucchi, *Three Dancing Nymphs and a Reclining Cupid in a Landscape*, ca. 1772, oil on paper, attached to a plaster ceiling roundel, the Metropolitan Museum of Art, New York.

p. 73, frumberdling: Frans Hals, *Young Man and Woman in an Inn*, 1623, oil on canvas, the Metropolitan Museum of Art, New York.

p. 75, fudgel: Peter Wtewael, detail of *Kitchen Scene*, 1620s, oil on canvas, the Metropolitan Museum of Art, New York.

p. 77, gardyloo: Jan Steen, detail of *Rhetoricians at a Window*, 1658–1665, oil on canvas, Philadelphia Museum of Art.

p. 78, gongoozler: Style of Adriaen van Ostade, *Man with a Tankard*, seventeenth century, oil on wood, the Metropolitan Museum of Art, New York.

p. 81, grimalkin: Auguste Renoir, *Woman with a Cat*, ca. 1875, oil on canvas, courtesy National Gallery of Art, Washington, DC.

p. 82, groke: Peter Paul Rubens, *Portrait of a Man, Possibly an Architect or Geographer*, 1597, oil on copper, the Metropolitan Museum of Art, New York.

p. 85, homerkin: Michiel Sweerts, *Man Holding a Jug*, ca.1660, oil on canvas, the Metropolitan Museum of Art, New York.

p. 86, honeyfuggle: Cornelis Bisschop, *A Young Woman and a Cavalier*, early 1660s, oil on canvas, the Metropolitan Museum of Art, New York.

p. 88, humbuggery: Peter Paul Rubens, detail of *The Meeting of Abraham and Melchizedek*, ca. 1626, oil on panel, courtesy National Gallery of Art, Washington, DC.

p. 91, humgruffin: Jacob Duck, detail of *A Couple in an Interior with a Gypsy Fortune-Teller*, ca. 1632–1633, oil on wood, the Metropolitan Museum of Art, New York.

p. 93, kickshaw: Severin Roesen, detail of *Still Life: Fruit*, 1855, oil on canvas, the Metropolitan Museum of Art, New York.

p. 94, latibulate: Eastman Johnson, detail of *The Hatch Family*, 1870–1871, oil on canvas, the Metropolitan Museum of Art, New York.

p. 96, love apple: James Peale, detail of *Still Life: Balsam Apple and Vegetables*, ca. 1820s, oil on canvas, the Metropolitan Museum of Art, New York.

p. 99, maffick: Giovanni Domenico Tiepolo, detail of *A Dance in the Country*, ca. 1755, oil on canvas, the Metropolitan Museum of Art, New York.

p. 101, mayhap: Jean-Siméon Chardin, detail of *The Scullery Maid*, ca. 1738, oil on canvas, courtesy National Gallery of Art, Washington, DC.

p. 102, minikin: Jean-Honoré Fragonard, *A Woman with a Dog*, ca. 1769, oil on canvas, the Metropolitan Museum of Art, New York.

p. 105, mumpsimus: Anthony van Dyck, detail of *Study Head of an Old Man with a White Beard*, ca. 1617–1620, oil on wood, the Metropolitan Museum of Art, New York.

p. 106, namelings: Raimundo de Madrazo y Garreta, *Girls at a Window*, ca. 1875, oil on canvas, the Metropolitan Museum of Art, New York.

p. 109, ninnyhammer: Jean-Siméon Chardin, *Soap Bubbles*, ca. 1733–1734, oil on canvas, the Metropolitan Museum of Art, New York.

p. 111, notekin: Italian (Lombard) painter, *Portrait of a Man in a Fur-Trimmed Coat*, ca. 1540, oil on canvas, the Metropolitan Museum of Art, New York.

p. 113, opscheplooper: Jan Victors, *Abraham's Parting from the Family of Lot*, ca. 1655–1665, oil on canvas, the Metropolitan Museum of Art, New York.

p. 114, pamphagous: Peter Paul Rubens and Jan Brueghel the Elder, detail of *The Feast of Acheloüs*, ca. 1615, oil on wood, the Metropolitan Museum of Art, New York.

p. 117, pelf: Rembrandt Harmenszoon van Rijn, detail of *Old Man with a Gold Chain*, 1626–1636, oil on panel, the Art Institute of Chicago, Illinois.

p. 119, pingle: Léon-Augustin Lhermitte, *The Grape Harvest*, 1884, oil on canvas, the Metropolitan Museum of Art, New York.

p. 120, popinjay: Daniël Mijtens, *Charles I (1600–1649), King of England*, 1629, oil on canvas, the Metropolitan Museum of Art, New York.

p. 123, prandicle: Pieter de Hooch, detail of *A Woman Preparing Bread and Butter for a Boy*, ca. 1660–1663, oil on canvas, the J. Paul Getty Museum, Los Angeles.

p. 125, prickmedainty: Thomas Sully, *Portrait of the Artist*, 1821, oil on canvas, the Metropolitan Museum of Art, New York.

p. 126, quafftide: David Teniers the Younger, detail of *Peasants in a Tavern*, ca.1633, oil on panel, courtesy National Gallery of Art, Washington, DC.

p. 129, quaintrelle: Henri Regnault, *Salome*, 1870, oil on canvas, the Metropolitan Museum of Art, New York.

p. 131, quanked: Charles Bargue, *A Footman Sleeping*, 1871, oil on wood, the Metropolitan Museum of Art, New York.

p. 133, quidnunc: Georges de La Tour, detail of *The Fortune-Teller*, ca. 1630s, oil on canvas, the Metropolitan Museum of Art, New York.

p. 134, ramfeezled: Joseph Wright, detail of *The Corinthian Maid*, 1782–1784, oil on canvas, courtesy National Gallery of Art, Washington, DC.

p. 137, rapscallion: Frans Hals, detail of *Boy with a Lute*, ca. 1625, oil on canvas, the Metropolitan Museum of Art, New York.

p. 139, rizzle: John White Alexander, detail of *Repose*, 1895, oil on canvas, the Metropolitan Museum of Art, New York.

p. 141, scambler: Joshua Reynolds, detail of *The Honorable Henry Fane (1739–1802) with Inigo Jones and Charles Blair*, ca. 1761–1766, oil on canvas, the Metropolitan Museum of Art, New York.

p. 142, scaramouch: Gustave Courbet, *Louis Gueymard (1822–1880) as Robert le Diable*, 1857, oil on canvas, the Metropolitan Museum of Art, New York.

p. 145, sciolist: Jan van Bijlert and workshop, detail of *Merry Company*, ca. 1630, oil on panel, the Walters Art Museum, Baltimore, Maryland.

p. 146, shivviness: Christen Købke, detail of *Valdemar Hjartvar Købke (1813–1893), The Artist's Brother*, ca. 1838, oil on canvas, the Metropolitan Museum of Art, New York.

p. 149, sloom: Gaspare Traversi, detail of *Teasing a Sleeping Girl*, ca. 1760, oil on canvas, the Metropolitan Museum of Art, New York.

p. 151, slugabed: Alexandre Cabanel, *The Birth of Venus*, 1875, oil on canvas, the Metropolitan Museum of Art, New York.

p. 152, smatchet: Frans Hals, *A Young Man in a Large Hat*, 1626–1629, oil on panel, courtesy National Gallery of Art, Washington, DC.

p. 154, snollygoster: Master of the Dinteville Allegory, detail of *Moses and Aaron before Pharaoh: An Allegory of the Dinteville Family*, 1537, oil on wood, the Metropolitan Museum of Art, New York.

p. 157, snool: Francesco Maffei, detail of *Hagar and the Angel*, ca. 1657, oil on canvas, the Metropolitan Museum of Art, New York.

p. 158, snuggery: Jean August Hendrik Leys, detail of *Dutch Interior*, ca. 1840, oil on wood (mahogany) panel, the Walters Art Museum, Baltimore, Maryland.

p. 161, somewhile: Francisco de Goya, *Bartolomé Sureda y Miserol*, ca. 1803–1804, oil on canvas, courtesy National Gallery of Art, Washington, DC.

p. 162, sonntagsleerung: Johannes Vermeer, detail of *A Maid Asleep*, ca. 1656–1657, oil on canvas, the Metropolitan Museum of Art, New York.

p. 165, sting-bum: Titian, *Doge Andrea Gritti*, 1546–1548, oil on canvas, courtesy National Gallery of Art, Washington, DC.

p. 167, tope: William Sidney Mount, detail of *Bar-room Scene*, 1835, oil on canvas, the Art Institute of Chicago, Illinois.

p. 169, tortiloquy: Jacopo Ligozzi, *Allegory of Avarice*, date unknown, oil on canvas, the Metropolitan Museum of Art, New York.

p. 170, uhtceare: Jean Honoré Fragonard, detail of *Diana and Endymion*, ca. 1753–1756, oil on canvas, courtesy National Gallery of Art, Washington, DC.

p. 173, ultracrepidarian: William Sidney Mount, detail of *The Tough Story—Scene in a Country Tavern*, 1837, oil on wood, courtesy National Gallery of Art, Washington, DC.

p. 174, verily: Sir Peter Lely (Pieter van der Faes), detail of *Sir Henry Capel (1638–1696)*, date unknown, oil on canvas, the Metropolitan Museum of Art, New York.

p. 177, waggish: Adriaen Brouwer, *Youth Making a Face*, ca. 1632–1635, oil on panel, courtesy National Gallery of Art, Washington, DC.

p. 178, wamblecropt: Alfred Stevens, *After the Ball*, 1874, oil on canvas, the Metropolitan Museum of Art, New York.

ABOUT THE AUTHOR

© NICOLE J. PERSUN

JOE GILLARD is the creator of History Hustle, an online history publication and Facebook page for the digital, mobile generation, and works in digital marketing. When he's not digging through historical facts, words, and anecdotes, Joe and his wife spend their time traveling, visiting museums and bookstores, and reading by the ocean in the Pacific Northwest.

For Nicole

Published in the United States by Ten Speed
Press, an imprint of Random House, a division of
Penguin Random House LLC, New York.
www.crownpublishing.com
www.tenspeed.com

Ten Speed Press and the Ten Speed Press colophon are
registered trademarks of Penguin Random House LLC.

Library of Congress Cataloging-in-Publication Data
Names: Gillard, Joe, 1983– author.
Title: The little book of lost words: collywobbles, snollygosters, and
    86 other surprisingly useful terms worth resurrecting / Joe Gillard.
Description: New York, NY: Ten Speed Press, 2019
Identifiers: LCCN 2019002616 | ISBN 9780399582677 (hardback)
Subjects: LCSH: English language—Glossaries, vocabularies,
    etc. | Vocabulary. | BISAC: LANGUAGE ARTS &
    DISCIPLINES / Linguistics / General. | SOCIAL SCIENCE
    / Popular Culture. | HISTORY / Social History.
Classification: LCC PE1449 .G447 2019 | DDC 428.1—dc23
LC record available at https://lccn.loc.gov/2019002616

Hardcover ISBN: 978-0-399-58267-7
eBook ISBN: 978-0-399-58268-4

Printed in China

Design by Debbie Berne

10 9 8 7 6 5 4 3 2 1

First Edition